ABANDONED SOUTHERN COLORADO
AND THE SAN LUIS VALLEY

JEFF D. EBERLE

America Through Time is an imprint of Fonthill Media LLC
www.through-time.com
office@through-time.com

Published by Arcadia Publishing by arrangement with Fonthill Media LLC
For all general information, please contact Arcadia Publishing:
Telephone: 843-853-2070
Fax: 843-853-0044
E-mail: sales@arcadiapublishing.com
For customer service and orders:
Toll-Free 1-888-313-2665

www.arcadiapublishing.com

First published 2020

Copyright © Jeff D. Eberle 2020

ISBN 978-1-63499-241-1

All rights reserved. No part of this publication may be reproduced, stored in a retrieval system or transmitted in any form or by any means, electronic, mechanical, photocopying, recording or otherwise, without prior permission in writing from Fonthill Media LLC

Typeset in Trade Gothic 10pt on 15pt
Printed and bound in England

INTRODUCTION

When we hear the name "Colorado," we envision the snow capped peaks of the Rocky Mountains, ski resorts, the bustling and vibrant Denver metropolitan area, and the Victorian-era gold and silver mining towns that have become popular summertime tourist traps. While all those places are Colorado, there is another Colorado south of the Arkansas River, which has a vibe all of its own. I have attempted to capture this unique part of Colorado through the photos contained in this book, but no set of photos or group of descriptions can truly convey the "feel" of this part of the state. It is somewhere you must visit on your own in order to truly appreciate it.

In terms of this book, "Southern Colorado" will mean the area south of the Arkansas River at Pueblo, to the New Mexico border, then all of the country south and east of Pueblo to the Kansas and Oklahoma borders. The Spanish Peaks and San Luis Valley will make up the western border of this work. Included will be sites in Pueblo, Huerfano, Otero, Las Animas, Baca, Costilla, Conejos, Alamosa, and Saguache counties. By no means can this be considered a complete work, for I have only scraped the crust of all that Southern Colorado has to offer.

Southern Colorado's history was built on a melting pot of cultures—Nomadic Native American tribes, Spanish explorers, French trappers and traders, Mexican settlers, Anglo cowboys driving herds from Texas, and Italian and eastern European miners. Southern Colorado just happened to be that spot on the map where all of these different cultures met and mingled, and today that history can be seen in the relics of yesterday that remain in the region, and can be heard in the voices and dialect of the people whose families have lived and intertwined here for generations.

When you cross over the Arkansas River at Pueblo, Colorado, you are crossing the old border into what was once Mexico prior to the 1848 Treaty of Hidalgo. Here, the architecture and culture abruptly take on a more Hispanic flavor. Place names here are more commonly Spanish, adobe walls and tin roofs replace the red brick and mortar of northern Colorado, and tiny Catholic churches and family cemeteries can be found in even the smallest of communities here.

This region also represents Colorado's coal belt—almost the entirety of the swath of land west of Interstate 25 at Pueblo, south to the New Mexico line just beyond Trinidad, and west to the foothills of the Rocky Mountains was coal-bearing. Numerous company towns, most owned by the Colorado Fuel & Iron Company, sprang up around the coal seams in the late 1800s, and thrived until around 1950 when the industry died. These coal towns brought in miners and their families from Italy, Greece, the Balkans, and the Slavic nations of Eastern Europe, with each of these cultures adding their own flare to the southern Colorado mix. And, lest we forget to mention Pueblo: the town was once billed as the "Pittsburgh of the West" with its gigantic smelters, steel mills, smokestacks, and railroad shipping yards that consumed so much of the coal from those nearby mines in the early years of the 1900s.

Sadly, today, those coal mines and steel mills are gone, and only the crumbling foundations of the worker's housing and the rusting stacks of the refineries and smelters remain. The sprawling rail yards at Pueblo sit empty, their once busy tracks rusting for miles in every direction. Nearly all the towns in the region have suffered decades of steady decline, and many have vanished completely, but their memory lingers on as an intrinsic part of the foundation that all of modern-era Colorado stands on today. Without southern Colorado, there would be no Colorado at all.

I hope, in some small way, the photos in this book can pay homage and give thanks to those hearty people who helped pave the way for the Colorado we love today. I hope this book causes someone else to stop and look at that old crumbling building in the distance, and see it as a reminder of what Colorado once was, and not just an eyesore that needs to be torn down and replaced with a strip mall or apartment complex.

In closing, I encourage others to take only photos, so that future generations can experience our past as well. A friendly reminder—removing items or vandalizing any historic site or structure over fifty years old located on public land is a felony in accordance with the American Antiquities Act of 1906 and subsequent legislation. This includes relic hunting, metal detecting, and salvaging/re-purposing operations conducted on public lands without state or federal approval. Enjoy Colorado's history—do not destroy it!

June 26, 2019

For hundreds of years Native Americans of the Arapahoe, Cheyenne, Ute, and plains Apache, as well as the Comanche and Kiowa, called southern Colorado home. At some point in the distant past, a member of one of these nations carved this image of a warrior into a sandstone wall in far southeastern Colorado. Sadly, modern man has felt the need to carve his name into the wall as well. Each year more and more of our nation's ancient history is defaced and damaged by people who think they need to leave their mark.

Above: Unnoticed by most, a sharp pair of eyes can pick out the form of a rock "hide" built by Native American hands. From here, hunters could watch over the canyon below for bison, antelope, deer, elk, and desert bighorn sheep.

Opposite above: A Native American recorded his first encounter with a horse into the Colorado stone hundreds of years ago. The appearance of the horse also signified the arrival of the first Spanish explorers to the region. The horse would change the lives of Native Americans forever.

Opposite below: The first well-documented Spanish expedition into the area that became Colorado occurred in 1593. Another expedition into the Spanish Peaks in 1541 was led by a Franciscan Priest named Fray de la Cruz but the history of that expedition is largely oral and part of local legend. Fray de la Cruz's party discovered gold and operated a small mine on Culebra Peak in the summer of 1541, before returning to Mexico that autumn. Between 1593 and the mid-1700s, at least a dozen Spanish expeditions explored the vast expanses of southeastern Colorado, the Spanish Peaks, the Sangre de Cristo Mountains, and the San Luis Valley to the west. By the late 1700s, seasonal bands of Spanish shepherds and ranchers would summer their herds in the lush meadows and river bottoms of the region.

7

It was not only the Spanish who signaled the arrival of the first Europeans in the area. French and English trappers and mountain men soon learned of the natural bounty of the area. Crude French maps dating to the late 1600s and 1700s detail the rivers and streams of the region, and accurately name and place the territories of the Native American tribes of southern Colorado. No permanent settlements were ever built by the trappers and traders. Only tiny cabins similar to this one in the Spanish Peaks marked their presence.

A sandstone pillar among the scrub contrasts with the arid prairie in Otero County, south of La Junta, Colorado. It marks the route of the old Santa Fe Trail, which connected Independence, Missouri, to Santa Fe, New Mexico, and was a major trade route between 1821 and the 1880s. Pillars like this can be found along the length of the old Santa Fe Trail, always within eye's distance of each other. Most have disappeared with time, but in remote stretches of the landscape, they can still be found. The Santa Fe Trail was, in essence, an early international commerce route connecting the United States and Mexico.

The very first permanent settlements in what became Colorado were in the far southeastern corner of the San Luis Valley in present-day Costilla County. When the region was still a part of Mexico, settlers from Santa Fe and Taos moved north in the 1840s into the San Luis Valley and settled along the Rio de Costilla, which flows through both Colorado and New Mexico today. Following the Mexican-American War, the 1848 Treaty of Hidalgo made these Spanish-speaking Mexican settlements part of United States territory. These adobe ruins in Costilla, New Mexico, were once part of Colorado until a surveying error was discovered in 1869, and Costilla was formally made part of New Mexico again.

With only two miles separating Costilla, New Mexico, and Garcia, Colorado, it is hard to tell where one community ends and the other begins. Adobe ruins dating to the earliest days of Hispanic settlement in Colorado can be found in all directions. In 1850, it was estimated that over 3,000 people lived in the Costilla-Garcia area of the San Luis Valley. Today, 200 residents live in and around Costilla and maybe a dozen or so remain in Garcia.

These tumbledown adobe remains in Garcia are among the oldest European structures in Colorado. Thick walls and the absence of windows are typical among the oldest adobe structures in Colorado. This was done for protection against both the weather and raids by Native Americans.

Garcia, Colorado, dating to 1848, was originally called "Plaza de los Manzanares" and was named after the family who settled the land. The old Mexican plazas were a cluster of thick adobe buildings arranged around a central square. Often adobe walls would connect each building, the walls and the buildings forming somewhat of a protective fortress for the settlers inside. Each little plaza across southern Colorado and New Mexico has or had a small Catholic church as well.

The Sacred Heart Mission in Garcia is typical of the Spanish style found throughout southern Colorado. These places of worship are still active today with congregations made up of the descendants of the original settlers, many of whom still own ranches and farms in the area. Please respect these places of worship when visiting as they are still a central part of life in these tiny communities.

Above: There simply are not words to describe the quiet, calm beauty of the San Luis Valley—it is truly one of Earth's special places.

Opposite above: Viejo San Acacio or "Old San Acacio" dates to the early 1850s and is a collection of crumbling adobe houses and a few occupied homes, which is typical of many of the small San Luis Valley communities.

Opposite below: Another long-abandoned adobe in Viejo San Acacio. As I was taking photos of this building, I noticed a family gathered for an evening meal on the porch of another home nearby. They all smiled and waved as I went about my business. The pace of life is slow here, and all the locals I have met in the towns of San Acacio and San Luis have been uncommonly warm and friendly.

Above: The Capilla de Viejo San Acacio is the oldest church in Colorado dating to 1856, a full two years older than the Our Lady of Guadalupe church in Conejos, Colorado, which often claims to be the oldest in the state. Like the Sacred Heart Mission in Garcia, the Capilla de Viejo San Acacio still hosts Mass and the feast day in honor of San Acacio. Tragically, in December of 2018, the church was vandalized and several thousand dollars' worth of damage was done inside.

Left: A window at the Capilla de Viejo San Acacio shows the distinct Spanish influence found across southern Colorado.

A tiny cemetery located on church property is the final resting place for some of the early residents of Viejo San Acacio. Stunning views of the snow capped peaks of the Sangre de Cristos mountains make a worthy backdrop for these pioneers of the San Luis Valley. The Spanish name "Sangre de Cristo" translates to "Blood of Christ" and the mountain range was named in 1719 by the Spanish explorer Antonio Valverde y Cosio, who was deeply moved by the reddish hue the snow-clad crags take on at sunrise.

Above: Just down the road from Viejo San Acacio is "new" San Acacio. Like its predecessor, new San Acacio has faded in the last century. With each passing season, this old farmhouse on the outskirts of town sagged closer and closer to the ground. Since this photo was taken in 2015, the building has collapsed and is now just a memory for those of us lucky enough to have seen it.

Opposite above: If an image could capture the heart of a region, I feel this shot of San Acacio does just that, with the old block general store, a forlorn Cadillac, and a seemingly out-of-place cross surrounded by immense natural beauty and blue skies that go on forever. The strong faith of the people of the San Luis Valley is symbolized by the cross, the general store which has withstood the ages is symbolic of the solid roots and deep history of the people, and the Cadillac is a symbol of more prosperous times in the valley.

Opposite below: Another angle of the general store in San Acacio. What stories could these walls tell?

17

In the charming town of San Luis, which dates to 1851, and is recognized as the oldest incorporated town in Colorado, this old general store stands guard beneath a surreal batch of summer thunderstorm clouds. San Luis is very much alive, but has a number of abandoned structures. Visitors come to San Luis every year to hike the Stations of the Cross sculpture exhibit created by local artist Huberto Maestas, which depict the final hours of Jesus Christ's life. The incredible sculptures and sweeping views from the mesa, as well as the stunning chapel at the top, are impressive to all who visit San Luis regardless of faith, and are a "must see" attraction while in the valley.

An old adobe, whitewashed and being reclaimed by nature at the tiny hamlet of Lasauses on the Rio Grande River. A few people still call Lasauses home, and like all the tiny settlements in the San Luis Valley, the church is the pride of the community. The name of the town comes from the Anglicization of the old Spanish "Los Sauses" which means "the willows." The descendants of the original pioneers of the San Luis Valley have a unique culture unlike modern-day Mexican or American cultures, due to the fact they have lived isolated in the San Luis Valley for hundreds of years, without major influence from either of their neighboring cultures. *Continued on next page*.

The people of the San Luis Valley have their own folklore and legends, and even some of the cuisine found in the valley is unique to itself. Though not as common today, many of the people still speak sixteenth-century Castilian Spanish, a dialect not spoken anywhere else in the world today, which owes its origins to the earliest Spanish explorers and settlers in the area. A popular saying in the valley is: "We didn't cross the border, the border crossed us," hearkening back to the 1848 Treaty of Hidalgo.

Main Street in Mesita, Colorado. Mesita was once an agricultural center and stop along the defunct San Luis Southern Railroad, a small, 30-mile-long spur off the main line of the Denver and Rio Grande Railroad—originating in Blanca to the north and terminating at Jaroso in the south—that opened the far southern end of the San Luis Valley to large-scale agricultural export during the first half of the twentieth century. The San Luis Southern Railroad was known as the "loneliest railroad in Colorado."

Mesita was once home to around 300, a number of whom were Mormons. Several homes and business buildings in and around Mesita are built from volcanic stone, which litters the prairie around the town.

There are a handful of abandoned homes lining the streets of Mesita. Their size and construction indicate that Mesita was once a prosperous place. When the San Luis Southern Railroad ceased large-scale operations in 1946, Mesita began to fade away. Today, Mesita is all but dead. A few buildings are used for storage of county road equipment and one or two houses are still occupied.

A volcanic stone farmhouse north of Mesita offers another glimpse of the immense beauty of the San Luis Valley.

Juan de Dio Ruybal settled an area along the Rio Conejos in 1856 and that place came to be known as Las Mesitas (not to be confused with Mesita, mentioned previously.) Today, not much remains at Las Mesitas other than the shell of the church which burned in 1975, and a small graveyard.

Built in 1919, this church replaced the original San Ysidro Church at Las Mesitias, which dated to the mid-1800s. By the time of the 1975 fire which gutted the church, the congregation had grown so small that rebuilding was not feasible, and just the picturesque walls have remained.

Hooper was founded around 1890 under the name "Garrison" and came to be because of the Denver & Rio Grande Railroad. A siding for the railroad as well as a small business district, including a bank and newspaper, grew at Garrison in the early 1890s.

A number of farms were established around Garrison, wheat being the top producer, but soon crops failed due to the alkaline soil and dry climate. The stock market crash of 1893 also hurt the fledgling community.

By the 1920s Garrison was nearly a ghost town, but railroad business kept enough people around that the town struggled on. The town changed its name to "Hooper," a moniker that it retains today. In the 1950s, the railroad line shut down, and Hooper once again declined. Hooper is a quiet place these days, with many abandoned and vacant buildings and just a few hearty locals who remain. A gas station on the edge of town serves tourists on their way to and from the Great Sand Dunes National Park a few miles down the road.

Moffatt was another of the small, early-twentieth century planned towns in the San Luis Valley designed to accommodate the needs of local farmers and ship their products to market. Like much of the valley though, the death of the railroads and the switch to gigantic corporate farms spelled the demise of Moffatt. The old city hall, on my last visit, was all but swallowed up by trees, and locals had painted demands to recall the city clerk on its side. A devastating fire swept through Moffatt in the winter of 2019 which consumed much of the business district, including this building, which was the oldest structure in the town.

When the last deposit was made at the Moffatt State Bank is difficult to say. Sadly, the old bank was another victim of the 2019 fire.

Another of the vacant buildings in the heart of the Moffatt business district that was likely lost in the fire of 2019. Of interest with this old building is the stamped tin facade piece featuring an intricate pattern. Fire, whether natural in the form of a forest or prairie fire, accidental, or arson, has consumed a tremendous amount of Colorado's early history in recent years.

In a scene straight out of the Old West, this picturesque, weather-beaten storefront can be found in the tiny community of Mosca in the San Luis Valley.

Another of the old stores in Mosca. It is hard to imagine, when visiting the town today, that it once had a hotel, school, flour mill, grain elevator, and railroad line, and boasted over a million bushels of wheat a year in production, but that was all before 1940.

On the very far northern end of the San Luis Valley, in Saguache County, where the valley itself comes to an end and the mountains rise again, a rich gold mining region was discovered by prospectors in the 1800s. North of the town of Saguache along a rough and rocky dirt road that few travel, you can find the ruins of Klondike, an 1890s-era mining camp named after the great Klondike Gold Rush of the Yukon that was happening concurrently at the time. Colorado's Klondike appears to have never amounted to much more than a cluster of log cabins and a few mine shafts though.

A collapsed cabin and scarcely detectable mine workings, reclaimed by nature at the Klondike site in Sagauche County.

This lone cabin stands along a dry creek bed about halfway in between Spook City and Bonanza in Saguache County. Beautiful in its surroundings, it must have been a lonely, isolated life for its long-forgotten inhabitant.

Early autumn skies frame the lone remaining building at Parkville, an obscure mining camp along Kerber Creek on the road to the more prosperous boom town of Bonanza in Saguache County. Today, the area around Parkville is used for ranching.

Perhaps the most photogenic house in the semi-ghost town of Bonanza, roughly 15 miles west of Villa Grove, Colorado. Bonanza has been an up-and-down mining center since the late 1800s, and is an eclectic mixture of occupied, abandoned, modern, and old homes today. Bonanza is a fun town to explore, and numerous 4 x 4 trails converge on the town from all directions. These trails will lead you deep into the mountains to mining ruins scattered for miles. Bonanza offers no services for those who visit, so plan accordingly.

Storm clouds roll in over another of the many picturesque homes in Bonanza that date to the boom days of the late-1800s and early-1900s. Bonanza is situated in a narrow valley along Kerber Creek, with numerous other valleys and gulches funneling in, most of which house mining ruins of some sort to explore.

On a steep hillside on the southern end of town, you can find the Bonanza Cemetery. Overgrown and hard to spot at first, the cemetery is the final resting place to many of the town's early miners and their families.

Nearly consumed after one-hundred plus years, this old grave can be spotted if you know where to look in the Bonanza Cemetery.

A simple board marks the resting place of a Bonanza miner, whose name is known only to the ages.

As you travel north up Kerber Creek past the town of Bonanza you will come to an open basin where the gigantic ruins of the Bonanza Mill can be found. Cloaked in green backed tar paper, this enormous stamp mill once processed the ore hauled in from the surrounding Bonanza Mining District.

Inside the Bonanza Mill is an impressive sight- An entirely wooden structure, featuring not a single iron or steel beam throughout. The remarkable craftsmanship of the structure is a testimonial to the carpentry skills of our forefathers. This mill building once housed gigantic cast iron stamp mill machinery and bins holding tons of ore. Without a concrete floor, or iron beam reinforcements, this all- wooden design handled unimaginable weight and stress loads, and is still solid today.

A staircase leads to the second level of the Bonanza Mill. The one handrail is a safety feature not found in many buildings of this era, and is now a government requirement in all modern-day factories, which require two.

Incorporated into the frame and walls of the Bonanza mill are shelves, cubbyholes, and desks where mill workers could store personal items, tools, etc.

One of two cabins left marking the spot of Exchequerville up the hill from Bonanza. Exchequerville had its own Post Office from 1881 to 1883 and a small, vibrant, community called the spot home, working the Exchequer Mine in the gulch above town. Floods have ravaged Exchequerville over the years, at one point exposing some of the bodies in the town's tiny graveyard. This cabin sits towards the top of a steep slope, and is surrounded by a field of sediment brought by the floods. Much of the rest of the town was washed away, or remains buried under the debris field.

A second cabin at Exchequerville can be found up the gulch on the trail to the Exchequer Mine.

Above: The tattered and forlorn remains of the Exchequerville Cemetery located up a steep trail above the town site.

Right: A child's grave at Exchequerville serves as a humbling reminder of the hardscrabble and often short, tragic lives of those who came before us. In the Colorado mining camps epidemics of disease, avalanches, floods, fires, and a lack of immediate medical access took a heavy toll on the populations, especially women and children, and every visitor to these old cemeteries will be taken aback by the disproportionate number of children's graves.

This house, which was clearly a gem in its day, can be found at the ghost town Russell at the western foot of La Veta Pass. Russell was named after William G. Russell, one of the founding fathers of Colorado, who discovered gold on Cherry Creek in the winter of 1858. Russell and his brothers went on to fame and were instrumental in the establishment of Denver, and the town of Russell Gulch near Central City. The Russell brothers left Colorado in 1862 to return to their native Georgia, where the formed a cavalry company that served in the Confederate Army during the Civil War. In the 1870s, Russell, his wife, and several other Georgia families returned to Colorado and discovered placer gold at the base of La Veta Pass, where the ghost town remains today.

This picturesque old adobe can be found at the Russell town site. After working his claim on the placer deposit for a few years, William Green Russell once again left Colorado and his fortune behind. An official government order decreed that all full-blooded Native Americans were required to live on Indian Reservations or in the Indian Territory. Russell was one-quarter Cherokee, and his beloved wife was full-blooded. Russell could not bear the thought of losing his wife to the government decree, so he moved to the Indian Territory (present-day Oklahoma) with his wife, where he died a few years later.

The forlorn remains of the diner at Up Top located at the top of La Veta Pass. Up Top dates to the 1870s and was a popular place for both train passengers and motorists to stop and stretch their legs up until the 1950s. When the new road over La Veta Pass was built in the 1950s, Up Top was bypassed, and became a ghost town.

Up Top has been listed for sale off and on over the years, and has about a dozen structures remaining. The third largest forest fire in Colorado history, started intentionally by an anarchist transient living in the United States illegally, consumed over 108,000 acres in the immediate vicinity of Up Top. Local fire fighters went to extraordinary measures to protect the ghost town, and only a couple of outlying structures were lost in the conflagration.

Though these buildings still remain at Up Top, today the surrounding hillsides are scorched black, a reminder of the tragic 2018 arson that burned for four months.

As you descend the eastern slope of LaVeta Pass from the ghost town of Up Top you will pass the site of Muleshoe and this old adobe boarding house. Muleshoe was named for a "muleshoe bend" in the tracks of the Denver and Rio Grande Railroad that once traveled over the pass and into the San Luis Valley.

The walls of an adobe dwelling from long ago stand defiantly in the face of time and the elements in the foothills of the Spanish Peaks.

Another abandoned homestead in the Spanish Peaks. The arid, rusty-colored terrain is a sharp contrast to the lush green grasses and dense evergreen forests of west-central and northern Colorado.

The quaint and remote community of Chama has a number of empty buildings, a few that are still occupied, and a small church. There are three places called "Chama" in this region, and it leads to some confusion. The largest and most famous Chama is in northern New Mexico along the Cumbres and Toltec railway. A second Chama is located a few miles southeast of the town of San Luis on the eastern edge of the San Luis Valley. Then there is the Chama pictured here, which is near Malachite and Gardner in the foothills of the Spanish Peaks.

A setting sun creates long shadows and captures the tranquility of a summer's evening at Malachite, Colorado, a small-time copper mining and ranching community. Pictured is the former combination Baptist Church and schoolhouse that served the town of Malachite and neighboring ranches. Today the building is used for storage.

This ornate tombstone blends in with the natural beauty surrounding the cemetery at Red Wing.

Since 1866 this Trading Post at Gardner, Colorado, has withstood the elements.

A tumbledown sandstone dwelling at Parras Plaza on the Purgatoire River marks the site of another 1860s-era plaza. In the early-1860s, thirteen families from Mora County, New Mexico, ventured north and traveled up the mouth of the Purgatoire River where it feeds onto the plains near Trinidad, Colorado. Along the way up the Purgatoire, each family stopped and built their own plaza bearing the family name. Today the plazas still exist. Parras Plaza was the northwestern most of the familial plazas founded in the 1860s along the historic route.

An old adobe structure, possibly a barn, near Parras Plaza on the dirt road to Vigil Plaza.

Another view of Parras Plaza. Descendants of the original Parra family still ranch the area, and as I passed through, I was greeted with smiles and waves from some cowboys mending a fence on their property.

A crumbling adobe and log house at the tiny community of Vigil, formerly Vigil Plaza.

This amazing adobe dwelling with lodge pole roof beams is perched precariously on a cliff overlooking a rushing creek below along the eastern edge of Vigil.

One of a number of vacant adobe houses at Vigil along Purgatoire River. Vigil is one of the few places in Colorado where there is still an active coal mine, and modern signs, equipment, and workings from the mine can be seen near the old plaza.

Like all southern Colorado communities, the centerpiece of Vigil is the Catholic church. Restored in recent years, this church has hosted countless services for the locals over the past century and is still in use today.

Weston, a small community along the Purgatoire River is a mixture of both old and new, occupied and abandoned. The general store has not seen a customer in many years, but still offers a colorful glimpse of Weston's former glory.

Above: The most unique building in Weston is this tiny adobe home, with accompanying outhouse, that would be at home in any Dr. Seuss book.

Left: Dating to 1871, and currently not in use, this fantastic church can be found at Medina Plaza on the Purgatoire River in the hills west of Trinidad.

Overgrown and surrounded by beauty, the church at Medina Plaza is a popular destination for tourists traveling down Highway 12, "Colorado's Highway of Legends," which runs west from Trinidad, then turns north just west of the Spanish Peaks and runs to Walsenburg.

Main Street in "new" Segundo, Colorado, another faded coal town west of Trinidad. What remains at the site, and is called "Segundo" on maps, is actually a much older town called Varros. The actual town of Segundo was located across the Purgatoire River from Varros and contained 145 cottages and 400 coke ovens for processing raw coal. Segundo was the largest coke processing town west of Chicago in the early twentieth century. Nothing remains of Segundo today. The ovens and cottages were bulldozed by the owners of Colorado Fuel & Iron when the coal industry collapsed in the 1930s and 1940s.

A Segundo/Varros family once called this fine adobe "home." Today, it is but a shell of its former self.

A red brick chimney slowly crumbles above the rusted tin roof of long forgotten Segundo/Varros dwelling.

A hard look at the faded paint reveals this old shop was once the Century Chevrolet garage at Valdez, Colorado. Today it appears to be used for storage.

Junk vehicles in a field near Valdez, Colorado. When the coal mining industry in the area faded between 1930 and 1950, many of the small communities west of Trinidad suffered and shrank to a fragment of their original size.

Another of the many scenic churches along Highway 12 in the Purgatoire River valley. This one can be found at the site of Tijeras Plaza.

Though they are weather beaten and faded by the winds of time, these are the final resting places of many of Colorado's earliest settlers, and are still sacred places to their ancestors who live nearby. Visitors should treat all graveyards with proper respect and dignity.

Right: Up and down the length of the Purgatoire River you will find similar tiny graveyards. Many of the burials are so old that the gravestones can no longer be read, and are in the process of returning to the earth.

Below: Angry summer skies frame the business district of Ludlow, Colorado. There is perhaps no other town in the region that more accurately symbolizes the struggle and tragedy of the Coal Wars of the early 1900s. On April 20, 1914, members of the Colorado National Guard opened fire on striking coal miners here. In the ensuing chaos, a bullet pierced a tent and started a fire that burned the miner's tent colony down. In the smoldering wake the bodies of 18 people, mostly women and children were discovered.

This impressive old building was rumored to have been a saloon. In the winter of 2018 the elements became too much to bare and the building collapsed. Today the toppled blocks are all that remain.

This building was supposedly a store and post office serving the town of Ludlow. On my last visit racks of wooden cubbyholes which held the mail for residents could still be seen through the window.

The old Ludlow schoolhouse and nearby teacher's cottage remain in a field of wildflowers against a backdrop of foreboding skies.

Rusted playground equipment and a naked flagpole next to the abandoned school stand as ghostly reminders of the children lost in the Ludlow Massacre.

This barn at Ludlow succumbed to the elements shortly after I snapped this final photograph.

As storm clouds roll across the prairie, a bird sits atop the remaining wall of a Ludlow home.

Plaque bearing the names of the victims at the Ludlow Memorial Monument. Tragically, most of the victims were children.

Just five short miles away from Ludlow is another tragedy town from the Coal Wars era- Hastings. All that remains at the site of Hastings today is a row of red brick coke ovens quickly being swallowed by the earth. But at the turn of the twentieth century, a sprawling coal mining complex and town covered this area. A mine explosion on April 27, 1917, shocked all of Colorado.

On the morning of April 27, 1917, a massive explosion rocked the valley where the town of Hastings was located. When the smoke cleared and the rubble was removed, 121 miners were found dead. A simple memorial marker sits in a field today as the only reminder of this tragic event, which happened almost three years to the day following the Ludlow Massacre.

South and west of Ludlow a short distance are the remains of Tobasco, another company town owned by Colorado Fuel and Iron. Not much remains at Tobasco today except for a couple of houses and shops buried in the trees and some old concrete mines structures.

Concrete mine buildings at Tobasco.

Just beyond Tobasco is the narrow entrance into Berwind Canyon, the site of numerous coal mines and company towns in the early days of the 1900s. Remnants of the mines and ruins of the towns can be found at intervals throughout the canyon, wherever a coal seam was found. Erosion in the canyon was a problem following the mining activities so junk vehicles and abandoned mining equipment were used to shore up stream beds and canyon walls.

More vehicles used to combat erosion in Berwind Canyon. The road through the canyon is actually the old **railroad** grade for the line that once hauled coal out of the numerous mines to Cokedale southeast of **Trinidad,** where it was refined in huge beehive shaped ovens which still exist today.

Concrete walls of worker's cottages pepper the hillsides throughout Berwind Canyon. Thousands of people lived and worked in Colorado Fuel & Iron company towns like this in the foothills of southern Colorado.

This sandstone stairway to nowhere once connected a railroad station platform to the worker's cottages and businesses located above the retaining wall. All the buildings were demolished when the mines closed so Colorado Fuel and Iron did not have to pay taxes on them. The miners and their families moved on with what little they had. Nature has overrun the town sites, and seemingly out-of-place reminders such as this are all that is left.

The company jail in Berwind Canyon. Yes, a company jail! Colorado Fuel & Iron had their own police force to keep workers in order. Those who got too drunk or rowdy, or caused political problems for the bosses, would be hauled off and thrown in the company jail indefinitely.

Refusing to topple without a fight, this three-walled house marks the site of Tollerburg, another Berwind Canyon coal town.

This red brick home near Tollerburg is unusual in Colorado's coal country, as nearly all the buildings and homes were made of gray cinder block, sandstone bricks, or concrete. The red contrasts greatly with the surrounding bland architecture.

The First State Bank of Aguilar in the Gianella Building dates to 1910 and closed its doors in 1927 as the coal mining industry fell on hard times. Aguilar was one of the larger towns in the coal belt and still hangs on today, though much of the business district is vacant.

An empty cafe in Aguilar's business district is a reminder of better times in the town, which is situated at the foot of the Spanish Peaks, and began its life in 1875 under the name of San Antonio Plaza.

East of the main business district this old building is said to have been the Aguilar grist mill during the boom years. Aguilar was a Hispanic settlement in its early years, then in the early-1900s, large numbers of southern and eastern Europeans moved to the town and worked in the plentiful coal mines nearby. Aguilar began to fade in 1930 as 200 miners lost their jobs when the Royal Fuel Coal Mine was shut down.

This picturesque home can be found on the eastern edge of Aguilar shortly before you leave the town limits.

All that remains of the coal town of Rugby is the general store. Thousands speed past this structure every day on Interstate 25 without even noticing it. Aerial views of the site show over fifty foundations scattered in the area west of the general store. An operating ranch sits on the site now, and there is no public access to the building.

An early twentieth century power plant built to serve the Walsen Coal Mine succumbs to time, vandalism, and illegal scrap metal salvaging. In 2009, the structure, which is a mile west of Walsenburg, was given protected status and a fence was built around the perimeter, but rampant vandalism still takes place.

A staircase leading to nowhere marks the spot where the YMCA building once stood at the coal town of Cameron south of Walsenburg. The hills around this staircase are littered with foundations and mining debris.

At the site of Gordon, Colorado, another coal town in the southern foothills near Walsenburg, the mine office and scattered debris are all that remain. The mine at Gordon ceased operations in 1937.

Coal mining structures that still stand at the Gordon site.

Some may remember Calumet, Colorado, as the setting of the 1980s film Red Dawn, but that was a work of fiction. Colorado's real Calumet was a coal mine and company town by the same name located northwest of Walsenburg on Highway 69. Mine operations began in 1904 and died out sometime in the 1930s much like the other coal towns of southern Colorado. The tin-roofed mine office, a barred off entrance to a shaft, and some concrete forms remain at Calumet today.

Tioga, like Calumet, is located along Highway 69 near Walsenburg. Tioga's life mirrored the boom and bust cycle of other nearby coal towns such as Calumet, Rugby, Tobasco, Berwind, and Ludlow. One building composed of numerous different kinds of sandstone blocks and bricks remains at Tioga as well as a huge coal tailings pile.

A glimpse through the trees reveals one of the few remaining adobes that mark the site of Badito. Badito was once the seat of Huerfano County in the early days of Colorado history. Badito sits on the spot where Juan de Ulibarri's Spanish expedition first crossed the Huerfano River in 1706, and in September of 1779, Juan Bautista de Anza, the governor of Nuevo Mexico, spent the night at the crossing after defeating the fierce Comanche Chief Cuerno Verde (Green Horn) in a battle nearby.

By the time Zebulon Pike explored the region in 1806, the Huerfano River crossing was well-known, and Pike too, found himself at the spot where the ruins of Badito remain. During the Civil War numerous southerners, leaving the mining camps of central Colorado passed through Badito on their way home to the southern states. In those days a rancher named Bo Boyce (Anglicization of the French name Beaubois) occupied the site and was sympathetic to the Confederate cause. Bo Boyce, a member of the secret Confederate underground network known as the Knights of the Golden Circle, would offer shelter, food, and arms to those secretly heading south to join the rebel cause. It is estimated that between 2,000 and 5,000 of Colorado's early miners and pioneers left to fight for the Confederacy during the Civil War. This high number was due to the vast number of Southerners who had come to Colorado in 1859-1860 during the gold rush.

An adobe schoolhouse, adobe hotel, the corral, and a historic marker are all that precariously remain at the site of Badito today. Each year the unprotected adobe walls crumble, and the weather-beaten planks of the corral rot just a little more. Soon nothing will be left of Badito.

Along Highway 69 west of Walsenburg, Colorado, a cluster of decayed buildings and a small Catholic cemetery mark the spot of Farasita. Farasita sits at the approximate spot of Fort Talpa. Fort Talpa was constructed in early 1821 by the Spanish, and was the northernmost fortification in the Spanish New World. Shortly after its construction, Mexico was granted its independence from Spain. The forgotten garrison at Fort Talpa was attacked by Native Americans of the Ute tribe, and the fort was burned. Fort Talpa lived and died under two different flags in one short year, 1821. Until the 1930s, locals claimed the adobe walls of the fort could still be seen on a bluff overlooking the confluence of Turkey Creek and the Huerfano River.

This picturesque church at Farasita now serves as a storage barn for farm equipment.

Greenhorn was once a roadside stop which included this diner. Sitting in a cool, shady canyon, Greenhorn must have been a welcome sight for weary travelers crossing the sun soaked expanse between Colorado Springs and Trinidad on the old Highway 85 in the early days of motoring. When interstate 25 was built, it bypassed Greenhorn by several miles, and today Greenhorn is just a sleepy cluster of houses and former business buildings.

The old service station at Greenhorn, Colorado.

Along Interstate 25 as you pass through Pueblo, you cannot help but notice the massive, semi-abandoned steel mill complex and rail yards that sprawl for over a mile.

Pueblo, Colorado, dates to the 1850s when it was a small Mexican settlement. In the latter part of the nineteenth century and into the mid-twentieth century, Pueblo was a huge industrial center, with numerous steel mills, smelters, refining operations, power plants, and railroad shipping yards.

Pueblo, Colorado, was once hailed as "The Pittsburgh of the West" due to its steel industry. But those days have passed, and now only small-scale steel operations take place in a few buildings in this massive complex. The rest of the mill lays dormant and decaying; soot blackened stacks, broken windows, and crumbling red brick remind us of hundreds of jobs that are no more.

Evening shadows and storm clouds frame this fantastic old barn and outbuildings on the far north end of Trinidad. Overgrown and left to the sands of time, this property sits next to the Las Animas County Fairgrounds on the west side of Interstate 25.

Ed's Tavern in Starkville, Colorado, is an impressive two-story sandstone block building in the heart of town. Starkville was once a major coal mining and shipping town in the early 1900s. Today Starkville is still a populated place, but has many interesting old and abandoned buildings to admire.

The old Methodist Church at Starkville as it sits today. The town manages to linger on unlike most southern Colorado coal towns due to its close proximity to Trinidad, where residents can access goods and services no longer available in Starkville.

One of the many old miner's shacks found in Starkville.

What looks like an old storefront lends a touch character to the dusty streets of Starkville, Colorado.

As you travel up the Colorado side of Raton Pass heading south toward New Mexico, you will notice a number of concrete foundations and the ruins of a mission-style church on the west side of Interstate 25. This is all that remains of the coal town of Morley. The rest of the town was bulldozed by the mine owners in the 1950s so they did not have to pay property taxes. When demolition of the church began, the bulldozer driver refused, stating that he, in good faith, could not tear down a church, so what was left remains today. Access is limited due to private property and a security guard patrol today.

Engleville in the shadows of the iconic landmark Fisher's Peak, near Trinidad, is an anomaly among southern Colorado coal towns. Engleville was not bulldozed, and a number of houses remain scattered among mining debris at the site.

An awesome stone house on the northern end of Engleville sits on the edge of a butte and gazes out over miles and miles of empty scrub-dotted prairie to the east.

A solitary sunflower adds life to the otherwise dead skeletons of Engleville.

This adobe chapel with its leaning cross can be found in Trinchera, an old railroad town about twenty miles east of Trinidad as you began the voyage onto the frying pan flats that is the southeastern Colorado prairie. Largely deserted, only a handful of people remain in Trinchera. No businesses remain open, and the old service station now serves as the local post office.

Cold beer was once a welcome reward for hot and dusty cowboys, and soot-caked railroaders that once stopped in Trinchera to stretch their legs and socialize.

Trinchera storefront.

A once fine home in Trinchera sports a design symbolic of the Spanish Peaks. A pair of mountains 13,000 feet in elevation, which have been used for hundreds of years by Native Americans, Spanish, Mexican, and Anglos alike as landmarks when traversing the region. The twin peaks can be seen for miles, and the Ute Indian Nation refers to them as the Wahatoya, or "Breasts of the Earth" where all life on the planet was born.

The old railroad station at Trinchera.

A buckboard wagon rots in the grass near a log cabin in Trinchera. It is unusual to find log structures in the land of adobe and sandstone block.

Another angle of a Trinchera storefront.

Model, Colorado, was a farming and ranching town dating to 1913, located along Highway 350, a 70-mile expanse of blacktop running diagonally northeast from Trinidad to La Junta, Colorado. Town planners viewed their community as "a model" town, thus explaining the unique name. Two rows of empty residential houses, this store, some garages, and another business building remain at Model today. Someone has recently purchased the old store and begun renovations.

Three of the residential houses at Model, along with a discarded 1950s-era refrigerator.

All the houses in Model are of a similar style. While looking around the town, a vicious dog came out of nowhere and charged me. I made it back to my vehicle just in time, but the dog then attacked it, jumping on the fenders and biting at the tires as I drove off.

A sign on a telephone pole nearby pointed the way and indicated this was the post office at Model, but I could see no signs of life or activity any time in recent years.

The schoolhouse at Tyrone, Colorado, along Highway 350, adequately illustrates the bleak, flat expanse of the southeastern plains.

Just east of the schoolhouse at Tyrone one can find this cinder block home. It is one of the few reminders that a town once stood at the spot.

A crumbling adobe building located at Tyrone appears to have once served as a radio station. Most small southeastern Colorado towns had one small building with a radio tower, a unique feature I have not found elsewhere in the state.

Thatcher was once a vibrant ranching, farming, and railroad town east of Trinidad, but the Dust Bowl of the 1930s took a heavy toll and the community never recovered. A two-story school, numerous foundations, and a few dilapidated homes remain at the Thatcher site today. It appears that someone is living in the schoolhouse.

One of the residential homes in Thatcher. The exposed adobe bricks on the front mean it will not be long until the elements topple this structure.

An isolated house along the road between Thatcher and Delhi. This image would seem to be more at home in the Texas panhandle than in Colorado, but the southeastern portion of the state has a very different look and feel that surprises many who think of Colorado only in terms of mountain peaks and pine trees.

Along the remote and vacant expanse of Highway 350 between La Junta and Trinidad, you can find the Delhi One Stop store. Long abandoned, the One Stop was once the main meeting point for local ranchers and people living in the tiny town of Delhi. Town planners wanted an exotic name for their locale, so they chose "Delhi" after Delhi in India.

Another angle of the Delhi One Stop. From a distance, it appears as if the station may still be in service, but as you approach, it quickly becomes clear that the building has long been abandoned.

These walls are all that remain of the general store at Bloom, Colorado, along Highway 350. Scattered rusty bits, foundations, and fence posts among the scrub-dotted hills mark the rest of the town site.

The two-seater outhouse at the Delhi One Stop: one door for men, one door for women.

Timpas—just outside of La Junta, Colorado, on Highway 350—is a ghost town with a number of remaining structures. One or two people still live there, but I have never seen anyone on my visits.

All that remains of San Joseville along Nine Mile Bottom southeast of La Junta, Colorado, is the remains of an old adobe saloon. Little was ever written and less is known about San Joseville. San Joseville was the home of Spanish-speakers who had settled the area from New Mexico sometime in the 1800s. Cowboys from Texas in the late-1800s running herds through the area would stop by the saloon for a beer and a game of pool. San Joseville faded and died as mysteriously as it had appeared.

Above: The Martinez Cemetery along Nine Mile Bottom south of San Joseville is home to a number of graves of former residents of the area.

Left: 1895 is the most recent date to be found on a headstone in the Martinez Cemetery indicating that San Joseville has been abandoned for longer than most Colorado towns have existed.

Kim, Colorado, is one of the few small towns that manages to hang on these days. Kim has a gas pump, a grocery store, and a new school to serve the largely dispersed ranching community of Baca County. The older part of Kim is almost entirely vacant, and all the streets in town are dirt. If you pass through, be sure to stop at "The Trail's End Bar" on the west end of town, and buy a beer from Helen, the delightful owner who can tell you all about the town's history.

Kim, Colorado, has more abandoned vehicles than it does residents.

A collector's dream awaits in far southeastern Colorado.

As you get deeper and deeper into the flat wastes of the southeastern Colorado prairie, signs of life begin to vanish, and, when you do see signs, such as Andrix pictured here, they have long been abandoned. This tiny store and a row of houses made up the town of Andrix, which served the needs of local ranchers. When the Dust Bowl hit southeastern Colorado in the 1930s, most of the farming and ranching operations suffered. Andrix dwindled as well. One old woman remained in Andrix until the early 1960s, running the store until she was robbed and beaten by a local man she had babysat when he was a child. After the robbery, the old woman closed the store, lamenting the fact that not even Andrix was safe anymore. Andrix has remained void of human life ever since.

All that remains of the town of Carrizo Flats today: a windmill frame, the platform and steps for the long-vanished bus terminal, a couple of swayback houses, a tree or two, and the stone walls and charred timbers of the schoolhouse. Carrizo Flats was born around 1920 and vanished shortly after during the Dust Bowl of the 1930s.

The stone block walls of the Carrizo Flats school, and charred timbers from the fire that burned the rest of the building.

One of the small homes that remains at the Carrizo Flats town site. Trees planted a hundred years ago are now just barely tall enough to provide shade and shelter from the Baca County heat and wind—a testament to harsh, dry climate, and lack of water in the region.

A mining town on the plains of southeastern Colorado? Yes. Carrizo City was its name. Around 1880, a band of flatlanders from Kansas set out for the mines of the Rocky Mountains in Colorado, and along the way they got lost. They reached the canyon country of Baca County, which skirts the New Mexico border, and assumed these must be the Rocky Mountains. They set out prospecting and managed to find some mid-grade copper ore along Carrizo Creek. A town composed of stone houses sprang up and people came to join the bonanza at Carrizo City. Carrizo City lived a wild and eventful life in the late 1800s, complete with saloons, parlor girls, and gunfights. Today, very little remains of Carrizo City. Sharp eyes can find a stone foundation here and there to mark the spot.

A short distance away from the Carrizo City site are the remains of a few stone houses in Carrizo Canyon along the creek bearing the same name. Desert Bighorn sheep can be found in the canyon, along with tree-lined, fish filled ponds at Carrizo Springs, making this a welcome oasis after endless miles of the flat, scorching, nothingness of Baca County.

Baca County in the far southeastern corner of Colorado which borders New Mexico, Oklahoma, and Kansas was the hardest hit county in the state during the Dust Bowl years of the 1930s. Many farmers and ranchers simply abandoned their homesteads and walked away, choosing to start over fresh somewhere else. Today, these scattered homesteads and ranches remain. Many are made of stone due to the lack of trees for use as a building material in this part of Colorado. A thick layer of baby powder fine dust, brought in by the Dust Bowl sandstorms, still blanket much of Baca County. Sparse scrub brush, cacti, and a few prairie grasses suck up what little rain falls on Baca County. Much of the county has been set aside as the Comanche National Grassland since it has lost all value as farm or ranch land.

Pritchett is one of three small towns in Baca County that manages to hold on. When the Dust Bowl ravaged the region in the 1930s, the population of Baca County dropped from nearly 11,000 to 6,000, and today the population has declined to less than 4,000 residents. Pritchett has a small business district, but all the shops and stores are vacant these days, and residents of the town must travel to nearby Springfield for necessities. Pictured here is the Pritchett Soda Shop.

Vilas, Colorado, can be found at the end of the shortest highway in Colorado—State Highway 100, which is less than one-half mile in total length! An abandoned business block and this old garage are just some of the sites to take in.

One of the shops along the overgrown sidewalks of the Vilas business district.

Vilas Town Hall, built in 1886, is rumored to have begun its life as a saloon in another nearby cattle town called Boston. Boston was said to have been a violent and rowdy town, straight out of an old Western movie. When Boston faded and died around 1900, residents of Vilas rescued the old saloon and moved it to their town. Today, nothing remains of Boston, Colorado, except for this building in Vilas, and a small cemetery a few miles to the southeast.

ABOUT THE AUTHOR

JEFF D. EBERLE, a native of Colorado, is a freelance writer, author, historian, and photographer. He has written two Colorado ghost town guidebooks, as well as *The Gray Ghosts of Colorado*, a book covering the sociopolitical climate of Colorado Territory during the Civil War, and *Abandoned Western Colorado: Ghost Towns and Mining Camps of the Rockies*. He is a regular writer and photographer for *Montana Ghost Towns and Beyond* magazine. Eberle has a blog at lifedeathiron.com, and he manages the Facebook page Colorado Ghost Towns and Historic Towns, which has over 6,000 followers. He hopes to share his passion for the preservation of history with others by engaging them through his photography.